The Vet

by Amy Jo • illustrated by Debbie Palen

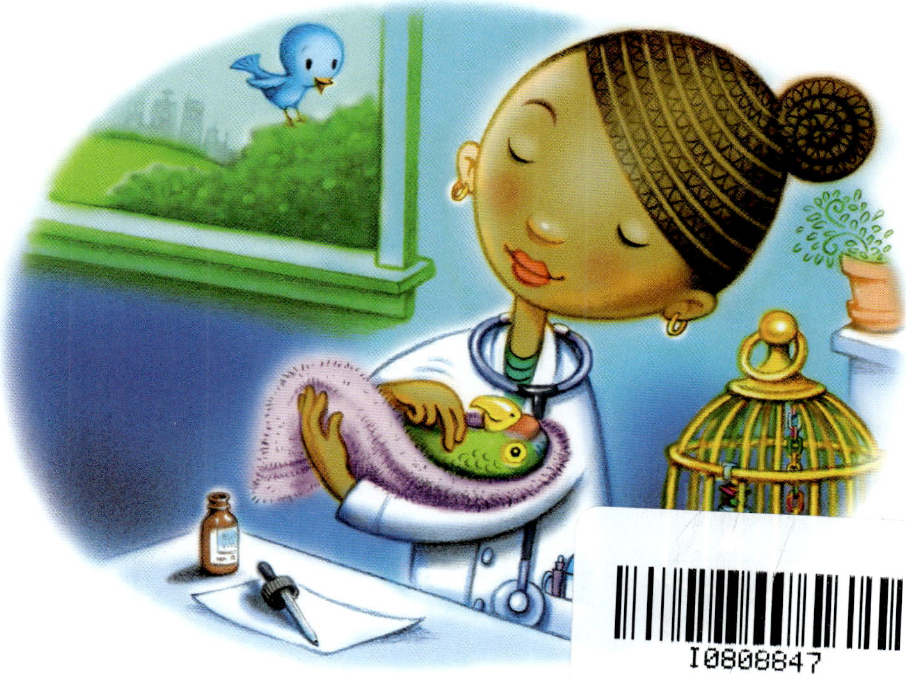

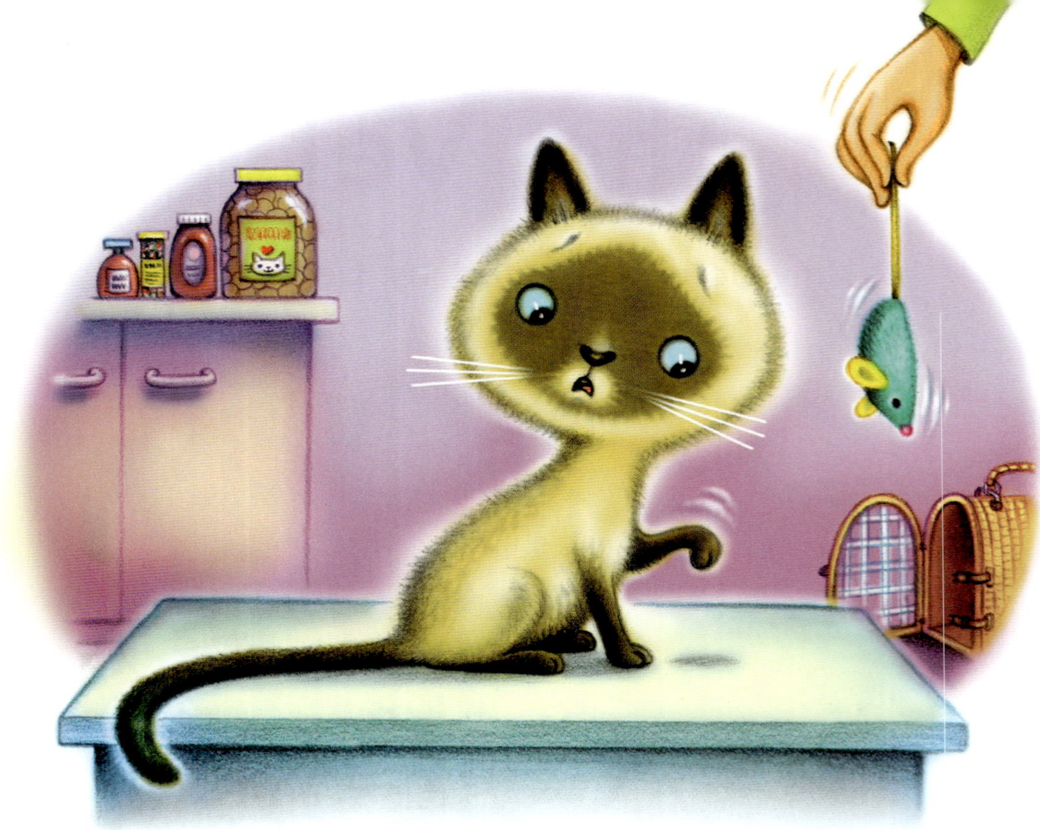

The cat can not play.

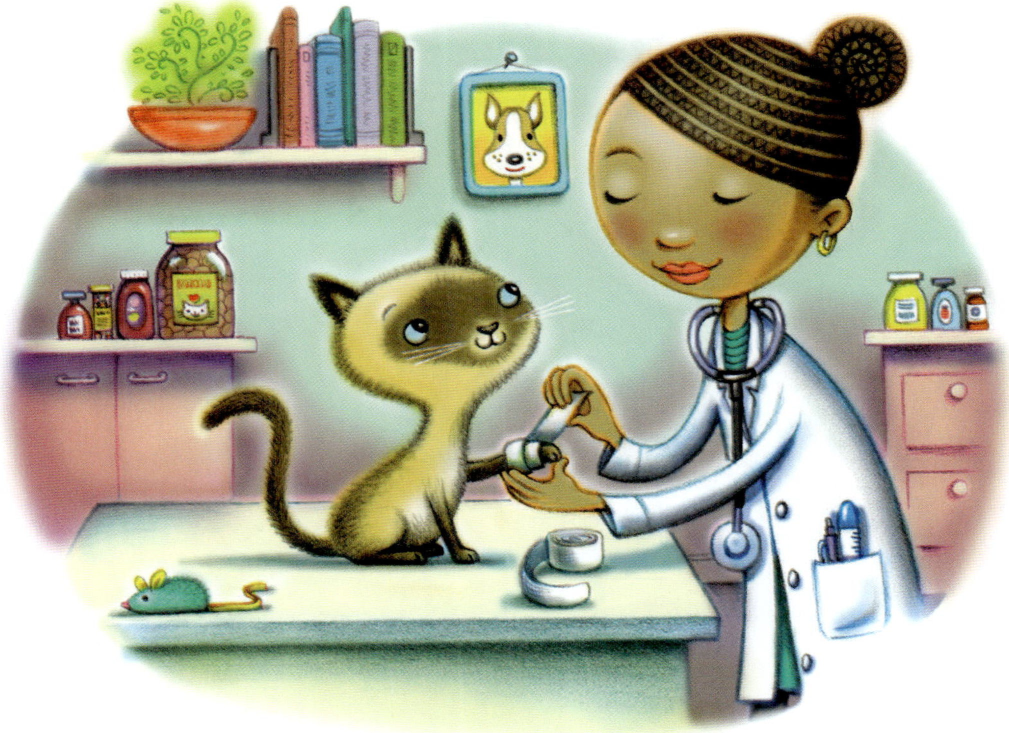

The vet can fix it!

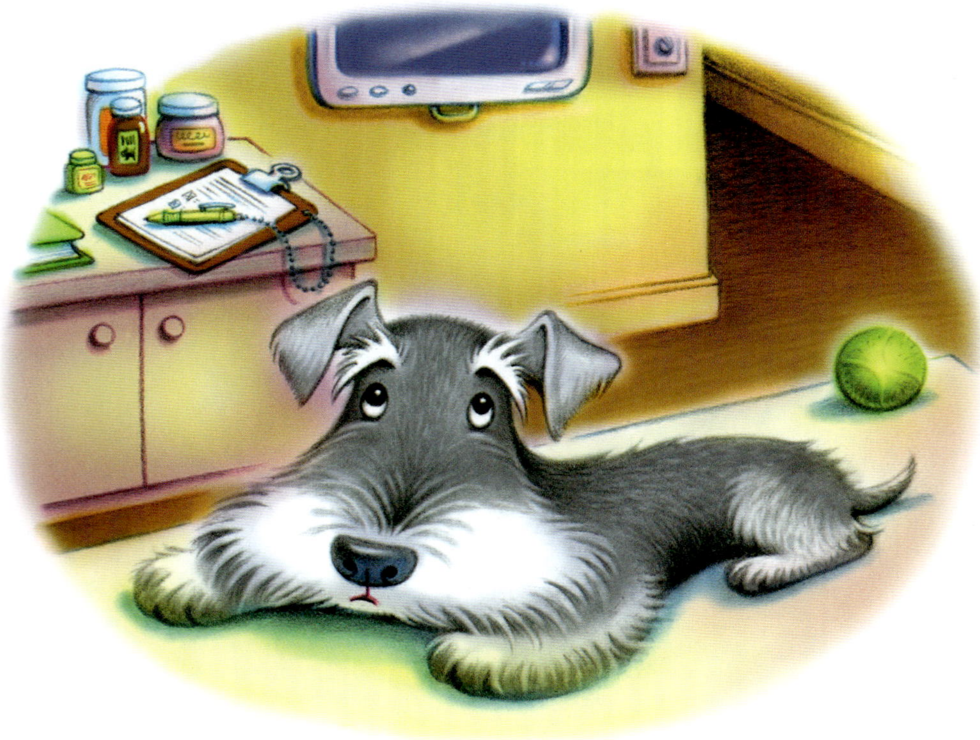

The dog can not play.

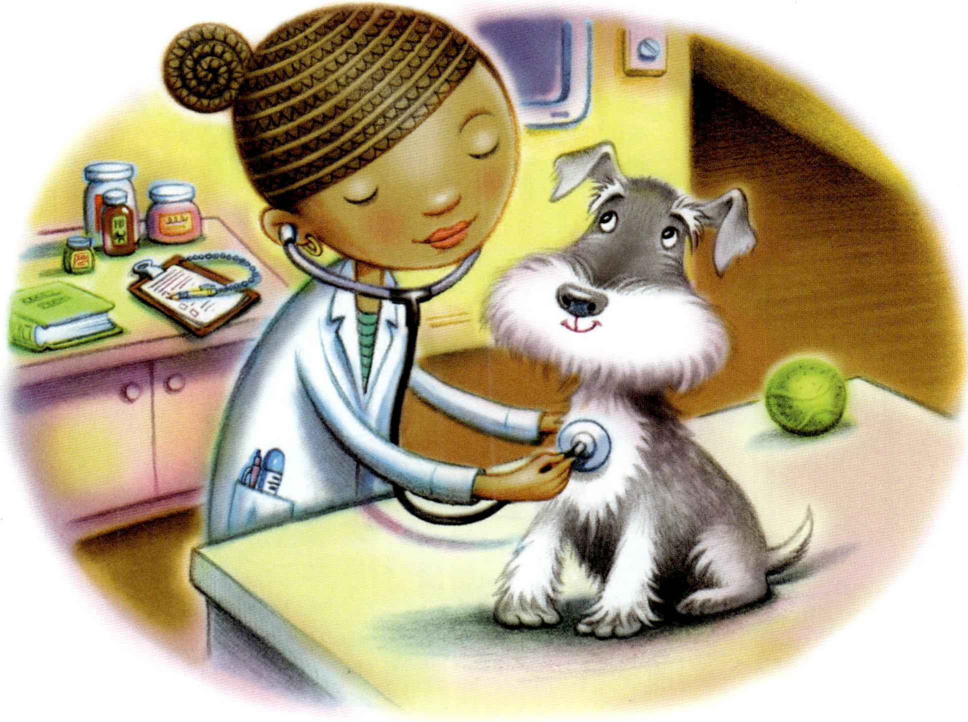

The vet can fix it!

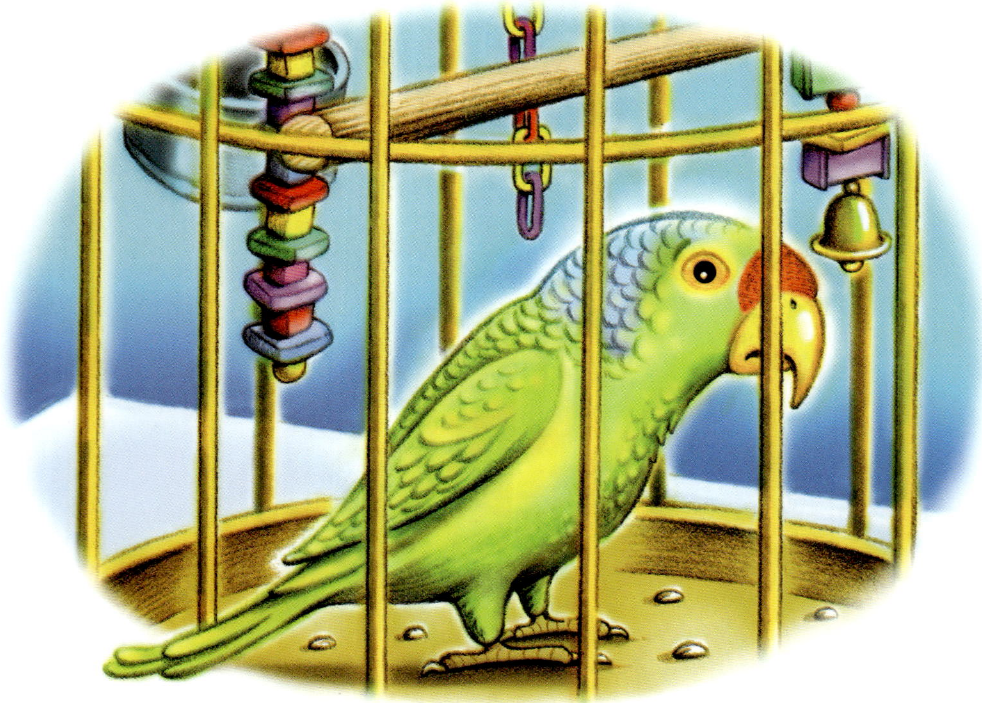

The bird can not play.

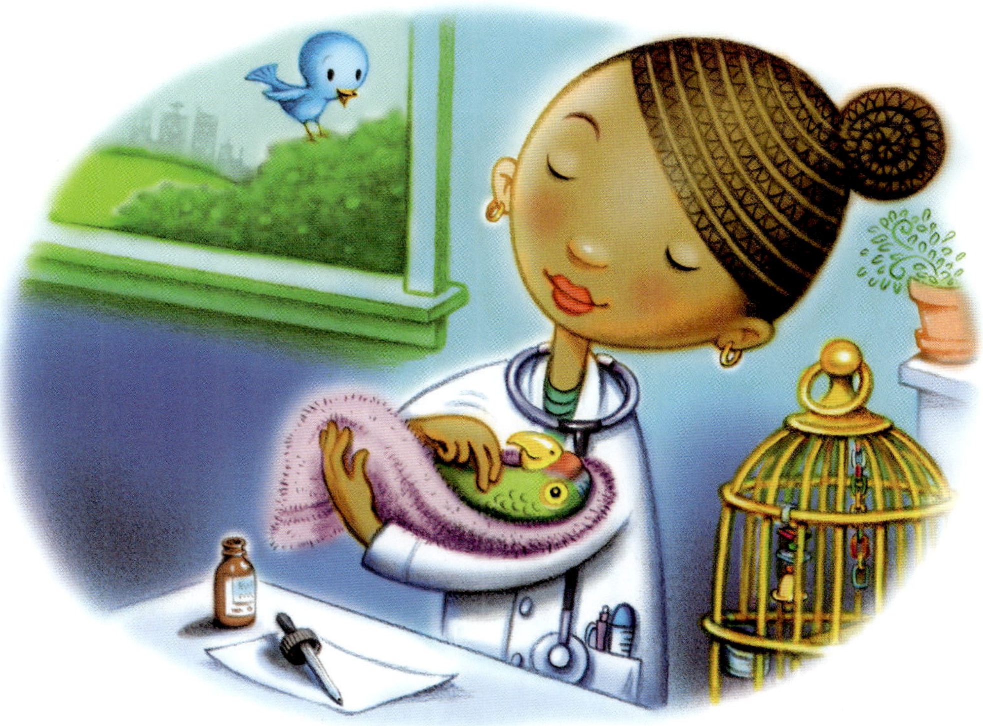

The vet can fix it!

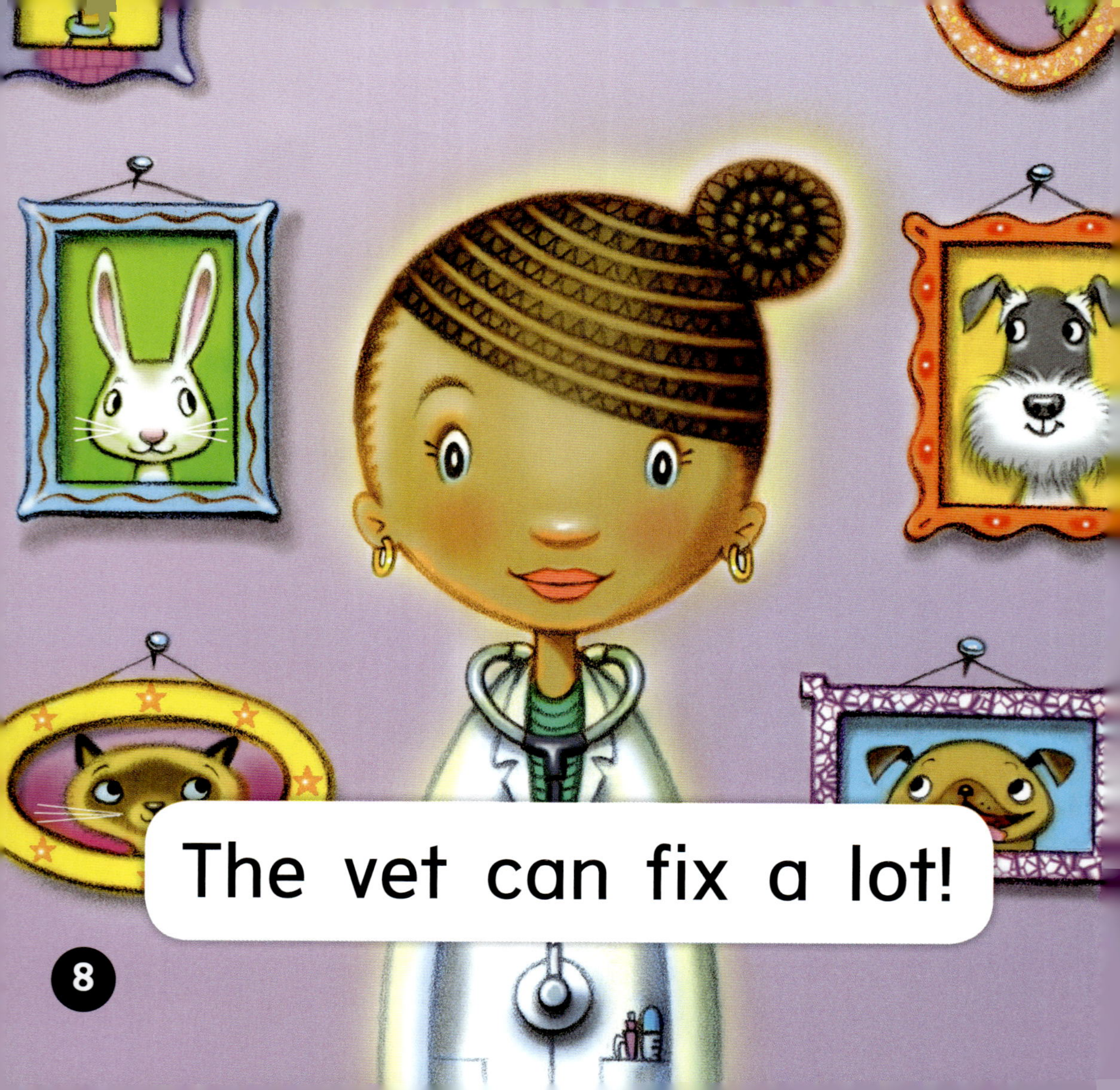

The vet can fix a lot!